DATE DUE

Breakthrough Inventions

INVENTING THE TELEPHONE

Erinn Banting

Crabtree Publishing Company

www.crabtreebooks.com

Crabtree Publishing Company

www.crabtreebooks.com

Coordinating editor: Ellen Rodger

Series editor: Adrianna Morganelli

Project editor: L. Michelle Nielsen

Designer and production coordinator: Rosie Gowsell

Production assistant: Samara Parent

Scanning technician: Arlene Arch-Wilson

Art director: Rob MacGregor

Project development, editing, photo editing, and layout:
First Folio Resource Group, Inc.: Tom Dart, Greg Duhaney, Sarah Gleadow, Debbie Smith, Adam Wood

Photo research: Maria DeCambra, Melody Tolson

Consultants: Peter Cowley, Deputy Curator, Telephone Museum, Milton Keynes, UK

Phil Goodwin, Curator, Telephone Museum, Milton Keynes, UK

Photographs: AP/Wide World Photo: p. 31 (top); AT&T Archives: p. 12 (top), p. 15 (left); Courtesy Bell Canada Historical Collection: p. 13; Bettmann/Corbis: p. 6, p. 7 (right), p. 11 (both), p. 12 (bottom), 14; Business Wire/Getty Images: p. 26 (bottom); Malcom Fife/Zefa/Corbis: p. 24 (left); Firefly Mobile/Getty Images: p. 25 (top); Garibaldi-Meucci Museum: p. 9 (both); Joanna Goodyear/istock International: cover (middle right); Granger Collection, New York: p. 16; Peter J. Jordan/CP: p. 31 (bottom); Matthias Kulka/Corbis: Pg 25 (bottom); Erich Lessing/Art Resource, NY: p. 4 (left);

Lucidio Studio Inc./Corbis: p. 23 (bottom); Rob MacGregor: p. 18 (bottom), p. 22, p. 29 (top);Mansell/Time Life Pictures/Getty Images: p. 10 (top); Mary Evans Picture Library: p. 17 (left); David Meharey/istock International: p. 29 (bottom); Dwayne Newton/Photo Edit: p. 26 (top); North Wind Picture Archives: p. 5; James W. Porter/Corbis: p. 28; Réunion des Musées Nationaux/Art Resource, NY: p. 4 (right); Science Museum/ Science & Society Picture Library: p. 7 (left), p. 8 (bottom), p. 10 (bottom); Science Photo Library: p. 23 (top); Michael Shake/istock International: p. 19 (top); Strauss/Curtis/Corbis: p. 24 (right); Telecommunications History Group: p. 17 (right); Geoff Tompkinson/Science Photo Library: p. 15 (right); Other images from stock CD.

Illustrations: Dan Kangas Illustration: title page, p. 3, pp. 20–21

Cover: Around for well over a century, telephones can be found in homes, offices, on street corners, and in peoples' pockets. The technology and appearance of this important invention have undergone many changes since the telephone was first introduced.

Title page: Most modern phones have push buttons with which to enter phone numbers. They also have handsets with transmitters, or mouthpieces, and receivers, or earpieces. Sometimes they have "hands-free" features, which allow people to speak and listen without handsets.

Contents page: Telephone handsets have devices, called anti-sidetone circuits, that prevent people who are speaking from hearing their own voices in the receivers.

Crabtree Publishing Company

www.crabtreebooks.com   1-800-387-7650

Cataloging-in Publication Data
Banting, Erinn.
    Inventing the telephone / written by Erinn Banting.
        p. cm. -- (Breakthrough inventions)
    Includes bibliographical references and index.
    ISBN-13: 978-0-7787-2815-3 (rlb)
    ISBN-10: 0-7787-2815-3 (rlb)
    ISBN-13: 978-0-7787-2837-5 (pbk)
    ISBN-10: 0-7787-2837-4 (pbk)
    1. Telephone--Juvenile literature. 2. Inventions--Juvenile literature.
I. Title. II. Series.
    TK6165.B36 2006
    621.385--dc22

                                    2005035442 770--dc22

**Published in
the United States**
PMB 16A
350 Fifth Ave.
Suite 3308
New York, NY
10118

**Published
in Canada**
616 Welland Ave.
St. Catharines
Ontario, Canada
L2M 5V6

**Published in the
United Kingdom**
White Cross Mills
High Town, Lancaster
LA1 4XS
United Kingdom

**Published
in Australia**
386 Mt. Alexander Rd.
Ascot Vale (Melbourne)
VIC 3032

Contents

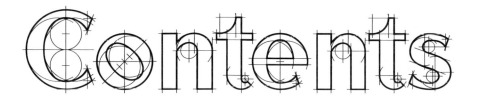

Early Communication

The invention of the telephone forever changed the way people communicate, making it easier to share information over short and long distances. Today, telephones are found almost everywhere in homes, offices, schools, and, with cellular phones, even in people's pockets.

By the 1800s, paper and ink had replaced earlier materials used to send messages.

Before Telephones

Long before the telephone was invented, people hired messengers to memorize messages and deliver them on foot. Around 3500 B.C., written language developed and letters were sent on pieces of bone, wood, or stone. In Egypt and China, from around 500 B.C., messages were written on animal skins, silk, and a lightweight paper called papyrus. These new materials made it easier for messages to be carried over long distances. Later methods of transportation, such as travel on horseback, allowed people to send and receive letters more quickly.

The rulers of ancient kingdoms used rock or clay slabs to send messages to their military leaders during battle campaigns.

The Pony Express was established in 1860 to deliver messages across the United States. Its first route ran 2,000 miles (3,220 kilometers) between St. Joseph, Missouri and Sacramento, California. Riders on horseback carried mail in stages, passing it to a new rider at the end of each stage.

Communication Signals

For thousands of years, people have communicated nonverbally, or without speaking. Some Native peoples of North America once covered fires with blankets in ways that created puffs of smoke that were different sizes and shapes. The smoke signals, which could be seen at great distances, were used to send messages, such as warnings about approaching enemies.

Some West Africans still send messages, such as greetings or blessings to neighboring villages, using talking drums.

Skilled drummers tighten animal skins that form the surface of the drums to create rhythms and **tones** that sound like human speech.

Semaphore

A system of communication called semaphore uses flags or flashing lights to send messages over distances. Code flags have been used since about 700 B.C. Each flag has a different symbol, which represents a letter, number, or message. Code flags are less common today but are sometimes used by ships that have lost radio contact.

The Telegraph

Telecommunications is the means of sending and receiving messages over long distances. In 1837, American inventor Samuel F. B. Morse discovered a way to send messages across wires. His invention, the telegraph, used an electric current to send signals between two locations.

Morse Code

Telegraph signals were transmitted in a code called Morse code. In Morse code, each letter of the alphabet was represented by a different combination of dashes and dots, which a telegraph machine recorded on a paper tape. Pushing a switch on the telegraph caused an electric current to flow across a wire. Depending on how long the switch was held down, a pencil attached to the **receiver** at the other end of the wire recorded a dot or a dash. The series of dashes and dots was then translated back into letters by a telegraph operator, so the message, or telegram, could be read.

Telegraphs in England

At the same time that Samuel Morse was developing the telegraph in the United States, Sir William Fothergill Cooke and Sir Charles Wheatstone were developing a telegraph in England. Their first telegraph model had two switches which, when pressed, sent an electrical signal to a receiver. The receiver had five needles that pointed to letters of the alphabet, depending on which switches were pressed and in which order. Cooke and Wheatstone's telegraphs were used for the next 80 years, although Morse's telegraph eventually became more popular because it was easier to use and more reliable.

Samuel Morse sent his first public message by telegraph in 1844. The message was sent along a telegraph wire that stretched 40 miles (64 kilometers) between Washington, D.C. and Baltimore, Maryland.

Telegraph Challenges

Inventors continued to look for ways to improve the telegraph. One way was multiple telegraphs, which allowed more than one message to be sent along a wire at the same time. In spite of these improvements, the telegraph had limitations. Sending telegrams required operators who were skilled in Morse code, which meant people had to go to a telegraph office to send messages. Sending lengthy telegrams was expensive. In 1850, it cost one dollar, or what the average person earned in a day, to send a ten-word message from New York City to Boston.

Cooke and Wheatstone's five-needle telegraph could not transmit the letters c, j, q, u, x, or z. Words that included these letters were spelled in unusual ways, such as "kween" instead of "queen."

Spreading the Word

By the mid-1860s, telegraph lines were laid in North America and Europe, and even crossed under the Atlantic Ocean. Businesses used telegraphs to place and receive orders, and journalists used them to send stories to newspapers.

Wealthy people sometimes had telegraphs in their homes for emergency use. These telegraphs were connected to a telegraph office. At the telegraph office, a light on the **switchboard** signaled to the operator which house a call came from, and whether the house required the police, fire department, a messenger, or a doctor.

Once reporters started to send stories to their newspapers by telegraph, news from around the world, which before had taken days or weeks to arrive, was available daily.

Sending Sounds

In the mid-1800s, inventors began to experiment with the idea of transmitting sound, including speech, over distances. Among these inventors was Antonio Meucci, believed by some to be the first to build a working telephone.

Science of Sound

The theory, or idea, of how sound travels has been around since at least the mid-200s B.C. Sound is a form of energy that is created when objects move. This movement creates a sound wave, or wave of vibrating air **molecules** that carries sound over distances. Sound waves travel at different speeds. The frequency of a wave is how fast it moves in a certain period of time. The faster a wave travels, the higher the pitch of sound. People can only hear a certain range of frequencies. Sound can be changed into other forms of energy. A sound wave can be turned into an electrical signal that can travel through wires, or a radio wave, which is another form of energy that travels in waves through the air.

(right) Later models of Reis's telephone had transmitters made from wooden boxes, and funnels covered with pigskin membranes, that people spoke into.

Early Telephones

In the 1850s, the German inventor and scientist Johann Philipp Reis began building a machine that he called a telephone. The word "telephone" comes from the Greek words *tele*, meaning "far," and *phone*, meaning "sound."

Reis built several different telephones that were all based on a similar design. He used the human ear as a model while building his inventions. His first telephone used a sausage skin in place of an eardrum, or the **membrane** inside of the ear that vibrates when it is hit by sound waves. A metal needle was used to act as the tiny hammer bone, which picks up the vibrations of the eardrum and sends a signal to the brain. Reis used an electric current to transmit the sound to the receiver. Although Reis was able to transmit sounds, he was never able to recreate clear speech.

Hearing Voices

Even before Reis' telephones, Italian-born inventor Antonio Meucci accidentally discovered a way to transmit voices over distances. While performing a medical experiment in 1849, Meucci put **electrodes** into the mouth of a patient and connected them by wire to an electricity-generating machine, which was in another room. Meucci also connected himself to the machine to make sure the current he was using was not too strong. When Meucci turned the machine on, he heard his patient's voice.

The Teletrofono

Meucci soon began work inventing a voice transmitting device he called a "teletrofono." Meucci built more than 30 models of the machine. One model consisted of two coils of loose copper wire, each in a heavy paper cone. The cones were connected by another copper wire charged with electricity. When a person spoke into the transmitter cone, the person listening at the receiver cone heard the vibrating airwaves as clear speech.

Demonstrating the Teletrofono

Meucci demonstrated the teletrofono in New York City in 1860. He hoped that people who saw the demonstration would provide him with financial support so that he could **patent** his invention. Unfortunately, Meucci was never able to raise enough money for a patent.

This wooden reproduction, or copy, shows one of Meucci's first teletrofonos, from 1857. The original was made of iron and steel.

Antonio Meucci immigrated to Cuba in 1835. He then moved to New York City in 1850 where he lived and worked until his death in 1889.

The True Inventor?

Scottish-born inventor Alexander Graham Bell is known to most people as having invented the telephone in 1876. Many people believe that Meucci's work makes him the true inventor. In 2002, the United States House of Representatives declared that Meucci's work should be recognized. That same year, the Canadian government officially stated that there was not enough information to support the declaration, and Bell was the true inventor of the telephone.

Bell's Experiments

Alexander Graham Bell was a teacher of the deaf and an inventor who experimented with the idea of transmitting speech over a wire. His research led to the further development of the telephone.

Teaming up with Watson

Many of Bell's experiments in the early 1870s involved improving the multiple telegraph, which sent more than one message along a single line at once. In 1875, Bell began to work with 18-year-old Thomas Augustus Watson, a skilled electrician at Charles Williams' Electrical Shop in Boston, where Bell bought many of his supplies. Bell had many ideas about how to transmit speech, but he needed Watson's help with the technical aspects of his inventions.

(above) Alexander Graham Bell, shown in the top row, first on the right, taught at the Boston School for the Deaf, in Massachusetts.

The transmitter of Bell's multiple telegraph is shown here. When a reed, or metal strip, on the transmitter vibrated, the matching reed on the receiver vibrated in the same way. Each pair of reeds sent and received its own messages, without interfering with other messages sent on the same wire.

Bell and Watson conducted their early experiments with telegraphs and telephones in a small laboratory in Boston, Massachusetts.

Transmitting Sound

On June 2, 1875, Bell and Watson were working in separate rooms, sending telegraph messages to one another. When Watson happened to pluck a reed on the telegraph, it vibrated and made a twanging sound, which Bell heard on the matching reed of his machine. It was the first time that Bell and Watson transmitted a sound.

Over the next year, Bell and Watson experimented with better ways to transmit sound. They used **diaphragms** created with membranes made of animal skin or metal, instead of reeds, and experimented with ways of strengthening the electric current that carried sound over a wire.

Major Breakthroughs

On March 10, 1876, Bell and Watson were experimenting with a telephone that looked like two megaphones, or cones. One was the transmitter and one was the receiver. They thought that speaking into the transmitter would cause its metal diaphragm to vibrate. The vibrations would be carried through a wire that had an electric current running through it, to the receiver. Then, the receiver would turn the electric current back into sound. Imagine Watson's surprise when, through his receiver, he heard Bell's call into the transmitter, "Mr. Watson, come here, I want to see you." Their telephone had worked!

When Bell spoke into the early transmitter, shown here, the vibrations caused the current in the wire to vary in strength as it flowed to the receiver. The varying current reproduced the changes in tone and volume of Bell's voice.

Speaking to the World

In 1876, Bell and Watson demonstrated their telephone at the Philadelphia Centennial International Exhibition. Scientists, inventors, businesspeople, and spectators from around the world came to the exhibition to learn about advances in technology. In the first public demonstration of their working telephone, Bell and Watson amazed and even frightened the audience, who could not figure out where the sound was coming from. Some people believed that the machine was actually speaking, not simply reproducing sound.

(right) Bell's telephone patent is one of the top patents, in terms of the amount of money Bell earned because of it.

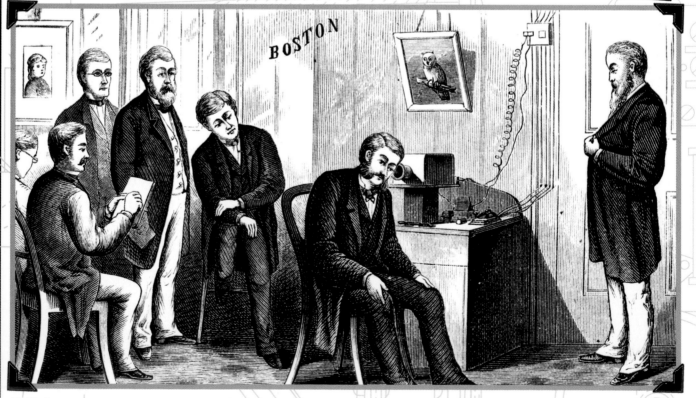

Bell demonstrates an early model of the telephone. To use this model, a person had to speak and listen through the same opening.

12

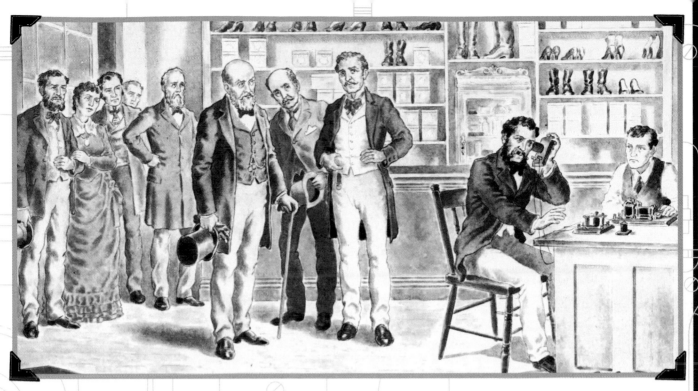

The First Long-Distance Call

On August 3, 1876, while visiting his family in Canada, Bell made the first long-distance call. Sent from the general store in Mount Pleasant, Ontario, the call travelled four miles (six km) to Bell's parents' home in Brantford, Ontario. The call was only one way: Bell spoke, while those gathered at his parents' home listened. Bell and Watson made the first two-way long-distance call on October 9, 1876, between the cities of Cambridgeport and Boston, in Massachusetts.

Bell's Invention

In 1877, Bell partnered with three **investors**, including Watson, to establish the Bell Telephone Company of Boston. The company installed telephone lines and rented telephone equipment to customers. At first, very few people wanted telephones because they were expensive, people did not understand how they worked, and few people thought they needed them. As the demand for telephones grew, the Bell Telephone Company spread throughout the United States and Canada.

On August 10, 1876, Bell made a second long-distance call. This call was sent to his parents' home from a store eight miles (13 kilometers) away. Bell used telegraph wires to transmit these first two long-distance calls.

Patent Controversy

Throughout his life, Bell went to court more than 600 times to defend his patent for the telephone and improvements to telephone equipment. One inventor who took Bell to court was Elisha Gray. On February 14, 1876, just two hours after Bell's application for a patent had been submitted, Gray submitted his own application for a similar patent. Each time Bell appeared in court, he won the case and kept his rights to the patent.

The Central Exchange

At first, a telephone line went to only one destination. People had to pay for several lines to connect them to more than one person or business. The central exchange put an end to the expense and confusion of multiple telephone lines by connecting all telephone lines to a single local switchboard.

The First Central Exchange

The first central exchange opened in New Haven, Connecticut, in January, 1878. Over time, more exchanges were built, and in the 1880s the first long-distance lines connected central exchanges in the United States. By 1915, telephone lines and exchanges connected calls between people in North America and Europe.

Making a Call

Early phones did not have dials or buttons. When a person lifted the telephone receiver to make a call, a light near a socket, or connecting switch, on a switchboard at the central exchange lit up. An operator plugged a cable into the socket to answer the call, listened for the name of the person the caller wished to speak to, then connected the other end of the cable to the recipient's socket, connecting the two lines.

Operators sometimes mixed up the lines they were trying to connect, and sent calls to the wrong people. The phrase "getting your wires crossed," which means to get the wrong message, originated from these mix-ups.

Early Switchboard Operators

The first switchboard operators were teenage boys who had delivered messages for telegraph offices. They were not used to speaking to the public, and often had poor manners. This led the Boston Telephone Dispatch Company, owned in part by Bell, to hire the first female telephone operator, Emma Nutt, in 1878. Within five years, most operators were women. To be a telephone operator, a woman had to be unmarried, and between the ages of 17 and 26. She had to look prim and proper, and have arms long enough to reach the top of the tall telephone switchboards. Working as an operator provided women with an alternative to being a servant or factory worker, but salaries and job conditions were still very poor. The average operator worked 11 hours each day, six days a week.

An engineer checks a telephone line in a modern automatic exchange, which is controlled by computer.

LIST OF SUBSCRIBERS.

New Haven District Telephone Company.

OFFICE 219 CHAPEL STREET.

February 21, 1878.

Residences.	Stores, Factories, &c.
Rev. JOHN E. TODD.	O. A. DORMAN.
J. B. CARRINGTON.	STONE & CHIDSEY.
H. B. BIGELOW.	NEW HAVEN FLOUR CO. State St.
C. W. SCRANTON.	" " " Cong. ave.
GEORGE W. COY.	" " " Grand St.
G. L. FERRIS.	" " " Fair Haven.
H. P. FROST.	ENGLISH & MERSICK.
M. F. TYLER.	New Haven FOLDING CHAIR CO.
I. H. BROMLEY.	H. HOOKER & CO.
GEO. E. THOMPSON.	W. A. ENSIGN & SON.
WALTER LEWIS.	H. B. BIGELOW & CO.
Physicians.	C. COWLES & CO.
Dr. E. L. R. THOMPSON.	C. S. MERSICK & CO.
Dr. A. E. WINCHELL.	SPENCER & MATTHEWS.
Dr. C. S. THOMSON, Fair Haven.	PAUL ROESSLER.
Dentists.	E. S. WHEELER & CO.
Dr. E. S. GAYLORD.	ROLLING MILL CO.
Dr. R. F. BURWELL.	APOTHECARIES HALL.
	R. A. GESSNER.
Miscellaneous.	AMERICAN TEA CO.
REGISTER PUBLISHING CO	*Meat & Fish Markets.*
POLICE OFFICE.	W. H. HITCHINGS, City Market.
POST OFFICE.	GEO. E. LUM, " "
MERCANTILE CLUB.	A. FOOTE & CO.
QUINNIPIAC CLUB.	STRONG, HART & CO.
F. V. McDONALD, Yale News.	
SMEDLEY BROS. & CO.	*Hack and Boarding Stables.*
M. F. TYLER, Law Chambers.	CRUTTENDEN & CARTER.
	BARKER & RANSOM.

Office open from 6 A M to 2 A. M.
After March 1st, this Office will be open all night.

The first phone book, published in Connecticut, was one page long and listed those people who had phones. Telephone numbers were not necessary, since operators connected all calls.

Automatic Exchanges

When exchanges were first introduced, it took operators as long as seven minutes to connect phone calls. Sometimes, they could only connect eight calls an hour. As the number of telephone calls increased, telephone companies looked for ways to connect calls directly, or without operators. The first automatic exchange became operational in 1892 in LaPorte, Indiana. Rotary phones, which are telephones with dials, were introduced at the same time.

Rotary Phones

When a person spun a rotary phone's dial, a series of electric pulses, or currents, was sent to the switchboard. The number of pulses depended on the number dialed. Dialing "5," for example, sent five pulses to the automatic exchange. When the exchange received the full telephone number, it connected the call to the correct line.

Selling to the World

The Bell Telephone Company controlled the patent for the telephone until 1894, making it illegal for other companies to manufacture and sell telephones until after that time. This did not stop others from trying to establish their own telephone companies.

Early Competition

The Western Union Telegraph Company, the largest telegraph company in the United States, hired American inventors Thomas Edison and Elisha Gray to build a telephone that their company could sell to compete with Bell's. In 1878, Bell **sued** Western Union for illegally using his patent, and won the case the following year. Western Union was forced to close its telephone division and give Bell the telephones and equipment it had built.

When Alexander Graham Bell's patent expired, hundreds of telephone manufacturers and service providers opened around the world. This illustration from the early 1900s shows a city street crowded with the lines owned by competing telephone companies.

Mind Your Manners!

Early telephone manufacturers had a difficult time convincing people to use telephones. Some people did not understand how telephones worked, and this made them feel uncomfortable. As well, people were not sure how to behave during telephone conversations. They often dressed up in fine clothing to make phone calls because they believed people on the other end could see them.

Telephone Greetings

People were unsure how to greet others on the telephone. Today, the polite way to answer a phone in many countries is to say "Hello." In the late 1800s, people, including Alexander Graham Bell, considered this greeting rude. Instead, people answered, "Hoy! Hoy!," the standard greeting used by sailors on passing ships.

The Cost of Making a Call

In spite of their lack of comfort with telephones, people discovered that making telephone calls was easier and cheaper than sending telegrams. Operators skilled at Morse code were not needed, and telephones were less expensive to maintain than telegraphs. Since people rented, rather than bought, telephone equipment, telephone companies were responsible for repairing the equipment at no charge to their clients.

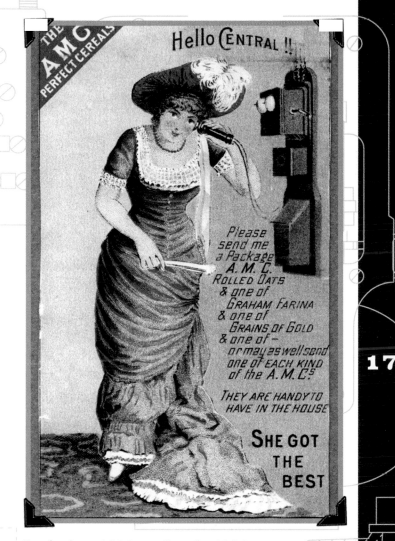

In the late 1800s and early 1900s, many postcards featured scenes of people speaking on telephones.

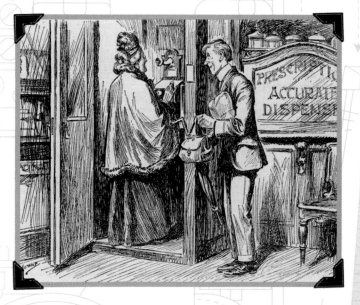

The first pay phone was introduced in Hartford, Connecticut, in 1889. In this illustration from 1913, a woman makes a call from a pay phone in a pharmacy, with the help of the pharmacy assistant.

The Party Line

The invention of the party line increased the popularity of phones in the 1920s and 1930s. As many as 20 people, or parties, who could not afford individual lines were connected to the same line. Each party had a different ring, so they knew if the call was for them. Party lines were widely used, but they were not always very private. People who shared the same line sometimes eavesdropped, or listened in, on other people's conversations.

Innovations

The first telephones were not easy to use. To make phones more popular, inventors built telephones that were simpler to handle and had better sound quality.

Ringers

In the days before the central exchange, telephones did not have ringers. A person making a call had to yell into the receiver, hoping that someone at the other end of the line would hear. The Bell Telephone Company attached the first ringers, invented by Thomas Watson, to telephones in 1878.

(right) Bell introduced the first phone with a separate transmitter and receiver in 1879, so people no longer had to listen and speak through the same opening.

Handsets

Handsets, which contain both the receivers and transmitters, were developed in Sweden in 1890, and became common in North America in the 1930s. With handsets, telephones became more compact. Manufacturers also began to use lighter materials, such as plastic, to make telephones, and they produced telephones in many colors.

When a person lifts a handset off a telephone's base, a switch is activated that opens a phone line, allowing the person to make or answer a call.

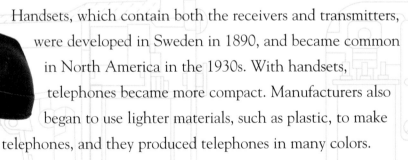

1837	**1844**	**1860s**	**1876**	**1878**
The five-needle telegraph is patented by Sir William Fothergill Cooke and Sir Charles Wheatstone.	Samuel F. B. Morse conducts the first demonstration of Morse code in Washington, D.C.	Giovanni Caselli develops the first widely used facsimile, or fax machine.	Alexander Graham Bell and Thomas Augustus Watson build the first working telephone.	The central exchange and the telephone ringer are introduced.

Touchtone Phones

Touchtone phones were introduced in 1963, making it quicker to dial numbers than with rotary phones. Touchtone phones led to the development of touchtone menus, a service that became widely used in the 1990s. Touchtone menus are computer systems that act as "receptionists," automatically directing calls to the appropriate people or providing anwers to commonly asked questions. These menus often include instructions on which buttons to press to hear certain information, such as a store's location.

Cordless Phones

Cordless phones were first used in homes and offices in 1989. Cordless phones allow people to move around when they are on the phone. The base of a cordless phone is connected by a cord and a **jack** to an outside phone line, but there is no cord between the handset and the base. Instead, **radio waves** carry signals between the two parts of the phone. The distance a person can move from the base depends on the strength of the radio wave signal.

(above) *When a caller presses a button on a touchtone phone, two different tones are sent to the central exchange. The central exchange's computer recognizes the combinations of tones that represent the telephone number, and connects the call.*

(top) *An antenna is connected to both the base of a cordless phone and the handset. These antennas receive the radio waves that carry the electrical signals created during a phone call.*

1892
The first telephone with a dial is introduced.

1894
Bell's telephone patent expires and competition in the telephone industry truly begins.

1940
Motorola releases the first walkie-talkie.

1946
The pager is invented.

1970
The first long-distance call is placed between London and New York without the help of an operator.

1989
Cordless phones are introduced for use in homes and businesses.

1993
The first digital mobile network, used to transmit cell phone calls, is built in the United States.

Parts of a Telephone

Telephones have changed over the past 100 years, but today's phones have many things in common with the earliest models. Most home phones have receivers, transmitters, dials or keypads, cords, and alerters. Some also have features such as built-in answering machines and call display **screens.**

1. Receiver: The receiver, or earpiece, receives electrical signals and changes them back into sound waves that are heard as a person's voice.

2. Transmitter: The transmitter, or mouthpiece, changes a person's voice into electrical signals. An amplifier inside the phone strengthens the signals before they are sent over telephone lines so they have enough energy to reach the receiver at the other end.

3. Handset cord: Handset cords connect handsets to bases, allowing electrical signals to move between the two parts. The first handset cords were straight. Curly, flexible cords were introduced in 1959. Stretching these cords allows people to move farther away from the base while talking on the phone.

4. Circuit board: The circuit board holds many of the telephone's electronic components, or parts. These parts are connected by copper circuits, or pathways, along which electric currents travel.

5. Alerter: The alerter makes a sound to indicate an incoming call. The first alerters, called ringers, were bells. Phones today are too small to hold bells, so they use **electronic** ringers.

6. Ringer control switch: The ringer control switch makes the volume of the ringer, or alerter, louder, softer, or turns it off.

7. Mounting cord: The mounting cord, or line cord, connects the phone to a jack in the wall. The jack is connected to outside phone lines, which connect the telephone to the **network**.

8. Hook switch: The hook switch connects and disconnects the caller from the telephone network.

9. Keypad: Buttons on a keypad have both numbers and letters. Until the late 1950s, some telephone numbers in North America consisted of both. The letters represented the area where a person lived, and the numbers corresponded to the person's line number. In 1960, telephone companies in North America began to use seven-digit numbers because they allowed for a greater amount of telephone numbers than the previous system of letters and numbers. Today, letters are sometimes used in a business' phone number to make it easier to remember, and a caller might press the letters of someone's name on a keypad to reach that person's telephone extension.

A Phone Call's Path

The telephone has made communication across any distance easier and faster. From the moment a person picks up a handset from its base, or presses the power button on a cordless phone, the process of making a telephone call has begun.

Calling Long Distance

When a person dials a local, or nearby, number, the call passes through one central exchange. Long-distance calls are more complicated. In the early days of the telephone, long-distance calls passed through many operators, including those at the caller's central exchange, in long-distance offices in the caller's city and in the city being called, and at the central exchange of the person being called. This took a long time. Today, the computers that control central exchanges store information about different routes that long-distance phone calls can take to reach their destinations. If one route is busy, the computer selects a less busy route.

When a call is made, an electric current, known as a ringing current, is sent along the telephone line and causes a telephone at the other end to ring. As soon as someone answers the phone, the ringing current is switched off and an electric current known as a speech current, which carries the speaker's voice, begins to flow.

Amplifying Phone Calls

A great deal of energy is needed to transmit long-distance calls so that a person's voice is clear and audible, or able to be heard. In 1894, Michael Pupin, an American inventor who was born in the former **Austrian Empire**, developed a loading coil, a device that amplified, or strengthened, electronic signals so that they could travel over distances. Later inventors developed other types of amplifiers that strengthened signals even more.

Analog and Digital Signals

Today, to improve the sound quality of phone calls, telephone companies use devices called modems to convert analog signals to digital signals. Analog signals are waves of electricity that once received by a telephone, are used to re-create a person's voice so that they sound the same over the telephone as in person. Analog signals lose power as they travel over distances, so phone calls can sound distorted or broken up. Digital signals are a type of electronic signal. They do not lose power as they travel over distances. Once a digital signal nears the telephone being called, a modem converts it back to an analog signal so the voice sounds like that of the speaker.

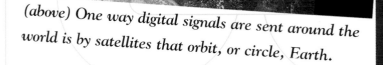

(above) One way digital signals are sent around the world is by satellites that orbit, or circle, Earth.

(below) Fiber optic cables that run beneath the ground, and even beneath the ocean, are used for both local and long-distance calls. The cables transmit more information than telephone wires, which helps make communication clearer.

Cellular Phones

As early as the 1920s, phones that used radio signals instead of wires were installed in the cars of traveling salespeople and later, in police vehicles. These early mobile, or cellular, phones led to the development of the cell phones used today.

How a Cellular Phone Works

Cellular, or cell, phones are similar to cordless phones, except that callers can move almost anywhere, as long as there is a cell tower nearby. Cell towers house powerful satellite dishes that transmit radio waves used by cell phones. When a person makes a cell phone call, a signal travels as radio waves to the nearest cell tower. From there, the signal travels to a central tower, and is connected to other towers, cell phones, or regular phones, which are known as landlines.

In remote parts of the world, where electricity and phone lines do not exist, cell phones powered by the sun are sometimes used.

Each cell tower receives signals for a small area, called a cell. As a cell phone user moves from one cell to another, the call is automatically passed to the next cell tower.

Cellular Phone Safety

Cell phones have made it easier and more convenient for people to communicate, but they have also caused health and safety concerns. According to some medical studies, there might be health risks for people who are exposed to cell phone radio waves over long periods of time. Using cell phones while driving can be dangerous to other drivers and pedestrians on the road.

This cell phone is made for children. It does not have a number keypad and can be programmed to only call certain numbers, such as those of parents or emergency services.

In some areas of North America and Europe, it is illegal to drive while using a hand-held cellular phone.

Changing Cellular Phones

The first cell phone was the Motorola DynaTAC phone, which became available to the public in 1984. The DynaTAC phone weighed 28 ounces (795 grams) and cost almost $4,000. Today, cell phones weigh as little as three ounces (85 grams) and are often given away for free by cell phone companies who want people to buy their services.

Customizing Cellular Phones

Users can now **customize** cell phones to suit their tastes. Faceplates of different colors can be clipped onto the fronts of phones, and many different ring tones, including popular songs, can be selected to let a person know someone is calling. Manufacturers have also developed special cell phones for children that glow in the dark and have flashing lights.

Part of Daily Life

The invention of the telephone not only changed the speed and ease with which people communicated, it also changed people's daily lives. Instead of traveling distances or relying on letters and telegrams, people use telephones to call friends and family, manage business affairs, find information, and get help in emergencies.

Dispatchers, or operators, at an emergency center take calls placed to 9-1-1.

Business Over the Phone

Business owners were among the first people to install telephone lines, since telephones made it easier for them to place and accept orders and answer customers' questions. Today, businesses that rely on telephones include telemarketing companies, which phone people at home and try to sell them goods or services, and polling companies, which survey people to find out their opinions on issues of the day.

Help Over the Phone

In emergency situations, telephones allow people to get help quickly. Dialing 9-1-1 in North America, or 1-1-2 in many European countries, connects people to emergency operators who send help from fire departments, police stations, or hospitals. If a person is too sick or in too much danger to speak, the operator can trace the call, or find out where the call is coming from, and send help.

Videophones allow friends or businesspeople to see one another while chatting or holding meetings, known as teleconferences, over the telephone.

Information, Please

Many phone numbers connect people to sources of information. In some communities, health-care professionals are available 24 hours a day to offer advice by phone to those who are sick. Help lines are available for children and adults looking for advice. Dialing 2-1-1 in some regions of the United States and Canada gives callers information about services in their communities, such as health and child-care facilities, and dialing 4-1-1 allows callers to find other people's telephone numbers. People can also dial special numbers to hear sports scores, movie listings, or weather forecasts.

Rules to Remember

Keep in mind these simple rules if you are on the phone with a stranger:

1. Do not give out personal information, such as your name, the names of family members, or your address.
2. Do not reveal your phone number to callers who think they dialed the wrong number. First, ask what number they dialed, then tell them whether they dialed correctly or not.
3. Do not tell callers that you are home alone. If they ask for an adult, tell them that no one is available at the moment.
4. If the caller says things or asks you questions that make you uncomfortable, hang up.

Misusing the Telephone

Telephones can be misused. Some people make crank calls, intended as pranks. Others call, pretending to be someone they are not, and ask for personal information. Callers may claim to be selling particular items. People interested in buying those items might give the callers their credit card numbers, only to discover that the callers used the numbers to buy goods for themselves. Many people today subscribe to services such as call display, which allows them to see who is calling before they decide to answer.

Today, people around the world are connected by more than one billion landlines and one billion cell phones.

Beyond Telephones

Advances in telephone technology have led to other forms of telecommunication. Fax machines, pagers, and personal digital assistants (PDAs) have allowed people to share information in new, more efficient ways.

Fax Machine

In the 1860s, Italian inventor Giovanni Caselli developed the first widely used facsimile, or fax machine. Caselli's machine, called the pantelegraph, scanned a page of words or illustrations, changed the print into electrical signals, and sent the signals over telegraph wires. The person at the other end received a facsimile, or exact copy, of the original document on his or her machine.

Modern fax machines use many of the same principles as early fax machines, but signals are sent over telephone lines rather than telegraph lines. Today, fax machines are not used as often as they once were since people are more likely to send documents by electronic mail, or **e-mail**.

TDD/TTY

TDD/TTY stands for Telecommunication Device for the Deaf/Teletypewriter. The machine, invented in the 1960s, allows people who are deaf or have difficulty hearing to communicate over telephones. The user types a message into the teletypewriter, which looks like a keyboard with a screen. Then, the TDD/TTY sends the message over a phone line. If the person receiving the call has a TDD/TTY, the message is displayed on the screen, but if the person does not have one, an operator connects the call and reads what the caller has written.

A woman uses a teletypewriter to send a message to her employer. Though they are still used, TDD/TTYs have become less popular as e-mail and text messages have become more common.

Family members use walkie-talkies when in large places, such as shopping malls and public parks, to communicate with one another if they are separated.

Walkie-Talkies

Walkie-talkies, or two-way radios, are devices that are set to a specific **radio frequency** to send and receive signals. The sender presses a button and speaks into the handset. The signal is transmitted by antenna to other walkie-talkies on the same frequency. Motorola introduced the first walkie-talkies in 1940, and soldiers used them during **World War II**. Today, couriers and employees in industries such as shipping, manufacturing, and retail use walkie-talkies to communicate at work. Some cell phones also have walkie-talkie functions.

Pagers

Pagers, originally called beepers, send messages over radio frequencies. Developed in the late 1940s, the first pagers beeped to notify people that there were messages for them. People then called pager operators to receive their messages. Today, callers dial pagers directly, key in their telephone numbers or text messages, or leave short voice mail messages. The pagers beep, vibrate, or light up when messages are left.

Computers and the Internet

The Internet is a network of more than 100 million computers that communicate and share information. People send one another e-mails and instant messages, which is like having a conversation except that people type in their messages rather than speak. People also browse **websites** to learn about topics of interest to them, watch videos, and listen to music.

PDAs

Some people have small, hand-held computers known as personal digital assistants (PDAs). PDAs serve as address books and daily planners. They also allow users to read, write, and edit documents, and connect to the Internet.

Some PDAs are combined with cell phones, MP3 players, and digital cameras.

In the Future

Technology is changing quickly. Many of the telecommunications devices now used are being replaced by new devices. Still others are becoming smaller, smarter, and faster. They are able to perform functions that no one would have dreamed of even a decade ago.

VoIP

Voice-over Internet Protocol (VoIP) allows people to make phone calls over the Internet. Their voices are converted into data that is sent through the Internet, just like e-mail. At the other end, the data is translated back into their voices.

There are many ways to make calls using VoIP, including using regular telephones with **adapters** that connect to computers or by speaking into microphones connected to computers. The main advantage of VoIP is that it reduces the costs of making telephone calls. For example, people who have Internet connections do not have to pay additional charges for long-distance calls. In the future, VoIP is expected to replace central exchanges and telephone lines.

Many cell phones take pictures, record videos, provide access to websites, send and receive e-mail, download music, and offer games.

Voice Recognition Software

Voice recognition software allows a computer to answer a telephone and seemingly understand what a caller is saying. The software translates the caller's voice into digital signals, then tries to match those signals against the computer's "dictionary" of signals. A person calling a telephone directory service might be asked by the computer, "What Yellow Pages heading would you like to search in?" The caller would say, for example, "shoe stores." The computer would then ask more questions to find out what area the caller would like to shop in; name shoe stores in that area; and give the phone number or other information about the caller's choice of store. As voice recognition software develops, computers will be able to interpret longer messages and recognize a broader range of accents.

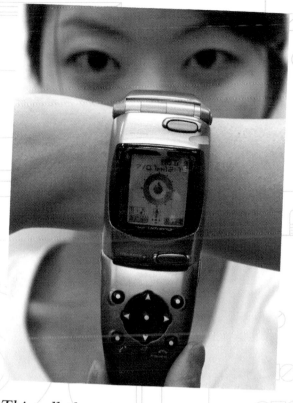

New Cell Phone Developments

Over the years, scientists and inventors have worked to improve the quality of sound that cell phones transmit and develop cell phones with different features. Recent innovations include cell phones that allow users to type in a company's name, or take a picture of the **bar code** on a company's product, then be linked, in seconds, to that company's website. Inventors are developing cell phones that do not interfere with radio frequencies that airplane pilots use to talk to air traffic control, so that passengers can use cell phones on planes. Inventors are also perfecting cell phones that translate conversations from one language to another, and tooth **implants** that pick up vibrations from cell phone calls, and transfer them to the inner ear. The tooth implant would allow a person to receive a call discreetly, or without others knowing.

This cell phone is worn around a person's wrist like a watch.

Radio wave signals travel from the tooth implant, through the jaw bone, to the inner ear.

Glossary

adapter A device that allows a piece of equipment to be used in a way other than that for which it was designed

Austrian Empire An area ruled by Austria from 1804 to 1867, which included the Kingdom of Hungary

bar code A series of vertical lines and numbers printed on a product that can be read by a laser scanner, providing information such as the product's price

call display A telephone service that displays the name and telephone number of the caller on a small screen on the receiving telephone

cellular A telephone system that uses radio waves to transmit voices and allows users to travel almost anywhere while still being able to use their phones

current A flow of electricity

customize To change something to suit someone's taste

diaphragm A thin disk inside a telephone transmitter or receiver that sound waves and electrical signals cause to vibrate

electrode A solid device that allows an electric current to be transmitted, or sent, into a non-metallic substance

electronic Related to a device, such as a circuit in a telephone or television, that uses electricity

e-mail A system for sending and receiving messages over the Internet

implant Something inserted into a person's body during surgery

investor A person who gives money to a company in exchange for a percentage of future profits

jack A socket into which a plug is inserted

membrane A thin, flexible piece of material used to cover something

molecules The smallest unit of a substance that can exist. Molecules keep the physical and chemical characteristics of the substance they make up

MP3 player A device that stores, organizes, and plays digital music files

network A telecommunications system connected by wires, cables, or other means so that people can exchange speech and information

patent A legal document that prevents people from using inventors' ideas for a certain period of time unless they give them proper recognition and payment

radio frequency A description of the range of electromagnetic waves that carry radio transmissions

radio wave A type of electrical energy used to transmit signals through the air

receiver A device that receives electrical signals and converts them into sound or pictures

sue To take legal action against a person or company who has done something wrong to get money or other compensation

switchboard A panel consisting of switches and jacks used by operators to connect telegraph or telephone lines

text message A short written message sent electronically to a hand-held device, such as a pager or cell phone

tone The quality and pitch of sound

transmitter A device that transmits, or sends, electrical signals or radio waves

website A set of pages about a particular topic that are linked to one another on the Internet

World War II An international war fought mostly in Europe and Asia from 1939 to 1945

Index